The Egham Picture Book

by

Dorothy Davis

Dedicated to the people of Egham, past and present

Published by Egham-by-Runnymede Historical Society
Text © Egham-by-Runnymede Historical Society
ISBN   0   9508234   3   0
Printed by Ian Allan Printing Ltd, Coombelands House,
Coombelands Lane, Addlestone, Surrey

INTRODUCTION

The photographs in this book are almost all from the collection in The Egham Museum, mostly donated or lent by local people and organisations over the years. Egham-by-Runnymede Historical Society is most grateful to them all. Of particular note are a number of excellent photographs, many of them commissioned by Egham UDC, taken by the late Mr F. Parkin, the Egham photographer.

The author owes particular thanks to those members of the Society who shared their research with her and helped to ensure, so far as is humanly possible, the accuracy of the text. We hope our readers will tell us more.

The Society is also grateful to Runnymede Borough Council for help and encouragement in the production of this book.

Dorothy Davis
August 1988

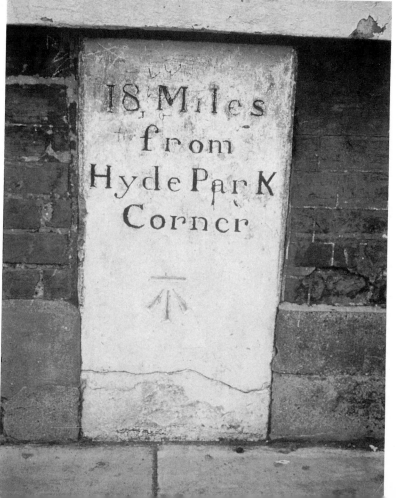

ACKNOWLEDGEMENTS

Acknowledgements are due to the searchers and researchers: Alan, Joan and Vivian Bairstow, David Barker, Mavis Collier, Ron Davis, Jim Godwin, Cyril Greenslade, John Hardaker, Desmond Mills, John Mills, Charles Sanderson, Vera and Vince Smith, Jill and Richard Williams and Ronald Wykes:

to the people of Egham who donated or loaned photographs or shared their memories: David Barker, Mr W. H. Beckingham, the late Mr J. Burt, Mrs D. Burt, Mrs D. Champion, Mrs Daborn, Mrs P. Doy, Mr and Mrs B. Dennis, Mrs Diana Fear, H. Fermor, W. Gilbert, Mrs Goode, Mr R. Hyde, Philip Lord, Mark Mitchell, Mrs W. Osman, the late Mr F. Parkin, Miss B. Parsons, Mrs I. Payne, Mr H. J. Pearce, Mr J. Pearcey, Mrs Pitman, Mrs Price, the late Mr W. J. Pummell, Mrs Nora Reeves, Mrs C. W. Southfield, Mrs Shreeves, Studio Egham, the late Mr A. Turner, Mrs F. Turner, Gordon Winter and any others inadvertently omitted:

to Croydon Public Libraries and Surrey Local Studies Library for photographs Nos 41 and 42:

to The National Trust for photographs Nos 95 and 96:

to the Royal Commission on the Historical Monuments of England for photographs Nos 15, 17, 34:

to Surrey Record Office for photograph No 4 and to Ken Simmons for printing from glass negative:

to Times Newspapers Ltd for photograph No 92:

to The Westminster Press for photograph No 33:

to Joan Hooper for manuscript typing:

to Joan Bairstow for lettering.

Where any possibility of copyright ownership exists, attempts have been made to contact the owner(s). Apologies are due if any do exist of which the publishers are not aware.

Egham-by-Runnymede Historical Society is a Registered Charity No 257294.

All proceeds from this book will go to further the aims of the above charity.

18 Mile stone in wall of 109 High Street, Egham.

P2355

THE VENTURE COACH AT RUNNYMEDE *c.1890*

In the 1890s the *Venture* drove from Charing Cross in London to Windsor via Egham in a nostalgic revival of the old coaching days. This is one of several photographs of Surrey coaching scenes, taken on glass plate negatives by H. Whittaker Reville. They were probably for use in his paintings of coaching scenes.

THE PACK HORSE *Egham Hill 1934*

Egham owed its prosperity in pre-railway days to the fact that it was a town on the Great Western Road, now the A30, linking London to Cornwall. Justices, members of parliament, soldiers, tradesmen and pedlars travelled on it: vagrants and beggars, hounded from parish to parish, sometimes died on it as the parish registers record. In 1807, Richard Wyatt of Milton Park and his son Edgell Wyatt of Englefield Green leased this inn for 60 years to Robert Porter and William Sutton Porter, brewers of Chertsey. It was to be insured with the Phoenix Insurance Co in London for £250 and the Porters had to 'purge, scour, cleanse and glaze' the premises within six months. The Pack Horse is thought to have been one of the oldest Egham inns. This building, situated just up the hill from the 19th milestone, was demolished in the 1930s, when the licensee was Mr Herbert Henry Poupard. Another Pack Horse was built which changed its name to the Royal Ascot in 1982.

P1383A

EGHAM HILL *junction with Middle Hill c.1906*

There was no shortage of public houses on the busy road from the west. Only 300 yards downhill from the Pack Horse was the Waggon and Horses fronting Egham Hill at the corner of King's Lane. The very names of these hostelries are evocative of their original clientele. A late 19th century Petty Sessions list shows them as entertaining 'respectable working men'. The Wagon and Horses was demolished in 1904 as being 'unfit for use'. The Castle, shown here proudly advertising its allegiance to the Friary Brewery in Guildford, was pulled down following the withdrawal of its licence in 1935. Its site is now only a grassy space. On the opposite side of Egham Hill, however, is still to be seen the forge used by the farriers and blacksmiths of the Castle: Forge Cottage.

Egham Hill, Egham.

P388A

EGHAM HILL *looking west c.1920*

As the London-bound traveller turned at the foot of Egham Hill towards the High Street, there was on his left yet another inn to tempt him from the highway. In the 17th century it was known as the Flying Horse; then its name was changed to the Running Horse. Finally it was given the name Eclipse after the famous horse that was born at the Cumberland Lodge stable in 1764, during a solar eclipse. The present Eclipse, rebuilt in 1935, stands further back from the road, the outbuildings having made way for car parking. Further up the hill was the Congregational Church, constructed in stone in 1851. It became redundant in the 1970s when its members joined the Methodists to worship as The United Church of Egham in what was originally the Wesleyan Memorial Chapel in the High Street. The old Congregational building was converted into a scientific instrument works and flats but has since become 10 flats. On the immediate left are to be seen the two villas built by William and Edwin Oldridge at the end of the 19th century. They carried out general smith's work there, repairing agricultural implements and acting as farriers. Their villas were demolished during road-widening in about 1967. An Aldershot bus can be seen on Egham Hill.

P91A

HIGH STREET *looking east c.1909*

The King's Head inn, the building covered in foliage, on the right, was a favourite place in the 17th and 18th centuries for gentlemen to meet, to dine and to rest their horses. In the days when traffic moved slowly on ill-made roads, travellers might stay overnight in Egham to avoid meeting footpads and highwaymen on Hounslow and Bagshot heaths. The advent of the turnpike roads and the faster mail coaches improved the standard and safety of travelling. Egham became a major stopping point on the London-West Country routes. In the 1820s *The Royal Clarence* coach travelling between London and Devonport and *The Magnet* destined for Weymouth stopped daily at this inn. The Hop Blossom was kept as a beer-house for many years towards the end of the 19th century by the widowed Ann Reeves when it catered for 'the respectable working class'. It closed as licensed premises in the 1930s. On the right-hand side of the picture are to be seen Henry Purbrick's hairdressing saloon and Tilt Brothers' bootmakers shop, which were cleared to make way for the shopping precinct in 1967.

THE CATHERINE WHEEL *High Street c.1895*

In the 17th century this was listed in a Parliamentary Survey as one of the principal inns of Egham. Trade tokens have survived from this period, bearing the tenant's name and the sign of the Catherine wheel. Thomas Rowlandson, the artist, visited the area in 1784. His water colour *Breakfast at Egham*, now in California, USA, is believed to show the interior of the Catherine Wheel. In the photograph the inn is seen as it was prior to its demolition in 1898, a stucco-faced early Georgian building under an overhanging tiled roof, with an imposing arched entrance for coaches, extensive stabling and an adjoining three-storey annex. It is thought to have been the oldest and was certainly the busiest hostelry in town, serving many of the long-distance coaches. In 1828, for example, 19 coaches a day were listed as stopping at the Catherine Wheel. Ostlers would be waiting in the inn-yard to see to the horses while servants provided refreshment for passengers and drivers. The first coach clattered into Egham at three in the morning, while the last one did not arrive until eleven at night. The High Street must have been a noisy place to live in, but this regular procession of coaches provided work for many of the town's inhabitants.

P370

HIGH STREET *looking east 1910*

With the coming of the railway to Egham in 1856 the coach trade faded. The Catherine Wheel was rebuilt in 1898 according to late Victorian fashion. At street level the annex, no longer connected to the inn, was transformed into shops. The Catherine Wheel retained its hotel trade but also catered for 'beanfeasters', employees on outings to Runnymede. The late-Georgian block of stucco-faced shops opposite included one selling teas which was popular with day-trippers on their way to the River Thames. This block was pulled down in about 1975. The shops on the left survive. The awnings that were widely used to protect shop window displays from the sun in the early part of this century are a distinctive feature. So also are the comparatively short dresses worn by the little girls and the ubiquitous hats. Hummer Road leading from the High Street alongside the inn to Runnymede was known in the 17th century as Little Humber Lane.

P1049A

COTTAGES AT THE REAR OF THE RED LION *1913*

Owned by the brewery, Friary Holroyd, the cottages on the right were 'empty and uninhabitable' in 1914 and soon demolished. The Red Lion itself was another old Egham inn that welcomed travellers off the Great Western Road. The *Western Hero* coach from London picked up passengers for Warminster, Frome and Wells on Tuesdays, Thursdays and Saturdays and returned from Somerset on the following days. One of the Southampton coaches, *Union*, sometimes used the Red Lion and the North Devon coach from Taunton always stopped at this inn on its way to London. From Taunton at that time it was possible to connect with a 'Branch Coach to Barnstaple and the Land's end (daily)'. In the latter part of the 18th century a social club made up of members of the local gentry dined at the Red Lion fortnightly. The membership was restricted to 20 but later increased to 25. In 1775 it included Sir Edward Blackett, the Reverend James Liptrott, Vicar of Egham, Thomas Sandby, the artist who designed the cascade at the head of Virginia Water, Dr Hugh Stephenson, the parish doctor, Serjeant-at-law Whitaker and Richard Wyatt of Milton Place. The latter, as well as being a local magistrate, was a member of the Trust of the Western District of the Bedfont to Bagshot turnpike road, which also met at the Red Lion.

P1284B

THE RED LION *High Street c.1908*

Attached to the Red Lion in the late 18th century and thus giving it greater importance were the Assembly Rooms. They were joined by a first-floor gallery running from the rear of both buildings. Egham Race Meeting Balls were held at the Assembly Rooms, that in 1785 being attended by HRH The Prince of Wales, later HM King George IV. In the early 19th century they were the setting for theatrical presentations, while during the rebuilding of Egham Parish Church divine service was held there. In 1845 the Assembly Rooms were sold for £750 and became 'The Literary and Scientific Institute and Public Reading Rooms'. Major reconstruction work occurred, financed by the sale of the former Red Lion skittle alley.

P389

HIGH STREET *looking west c.1908*

A large hall at the rear of the Literary Institute and a Dispensary underneath the gallery were added between 1857 and 1859. From the 1880s until the 1920s local doctors attended the Dispensary between 9-10am on Tuesdays, Wednesdays, Fridays and Saturdays. The Dispensary and gallery were removed in the 1930s. Interesting architectural features of the building are the simulated stonework at the base of the front façade and the lettering LITERARY INSTITUTE moulded into the stucco. The bricked-in windows may reflect a desire for symmetry or may be the result of internal rearrangement of rooms. The building is still used by many Egham clubs and societies. Runnymede Drama Group regularly presents amateur dramatics in the hall, and the old Assembly Rooms have housed The Egham Museum, run on a voluntary basis, assisted by members of Egham-by-Runnymede Historical Society, since 1968.

P693A

DANCE AT THE LITERARY INSTITUTE *during the Second World War, 1939-45*

During the Second World War social events were still held in the hall, the Union flags and bunting reflecting the patriotic feeling of the time. Servicemen on leave joined with civilians, some of them munitions workers from Petters, in a precious few hours of relaxation from wartime pressures. The caretaker at the time, Mrs Brown, is to be seen third from the left in the back row. The under-croft of the old building served additionally as an air raid shelter. Protective sand that was then placed under the floor boards was removed during the 1980s renovations.

P1145

EGHAM PARISH CHURCH: ST JOHN THE BAPTIST *c.1944*

The 'new church' of Egham dates from 1820, the first service being held there on 16 March. The designer was Henry Rhodes and the building work was undertaken by Robert Pinney of Pimlico at an original estimate of £6,155. The final bill, however, with all the additions and refinements, was nearer £8,000. It was built in the neo-classical style popular in the early 19th century but its interior is spacious and well proportioned, with many memorials from the earlier church being transferred to the new building. An unusual feature is a series of vaults or catacombs which were built in the crypt and which were advertised for sale. The new church did not find favour with everyone. The Reverend Dr John Samuel Bewley Monsell, the famous hymn writer, who was Vicar of Egham from 1853 to 1870 wrote: 'My parish church is so bad in form and feature that its influence must be, no matter how people struggle against it, to unsolemnise.' Dr Monsell was the writer of such popular hymns as 'Fight the Good Fight'.

P1778

THE LYCH GATE OF THE PRESENT EGHAM CHURCH

This had been the entrance porch of the north door of the old church. It was removed about 1817 when the old church, dating from the 12th century was demolished. At a parish meeting in April 1814 consideration was given to 'the ruinous and inconvenient state of the parish church'. A committee was appointed and plans were drawn up for either the renovation of the old church or the building of a new one. Two months later at a further committee meeting, all ideas of renovating the old church had vanished. Some remains of the old church, including a fine Norman arch and a piscina, can be seen in the grounds of Milton Park. A plaque under the lych gate records a visit by John Wesley in 1743. Wesley was not impressed by the priest, probably the Reverend Thomas Beighton, who gave the sermon. The lych gate was placed in its present position in 1938, having been for many years in the garden of a house in Bakeham Lane. It was completely renovated in 1986.

DENHAM'S MONUMENT TO HIS TWO WIVES *Egham Church*

Sir John Denham, Justice and Baron of the Exchequer was one of Egham's benefactors. He first came to the district at the end of the 16th century and was buried in Egham in January 1638. A fine monument to his memory survives in the present Parish Church, as does his memorial to his two wives. The latter includes a tiny statue of his son, also John, the future poet who was to commemorate in verse the view from Cooper's Hill overlooking the Thames at Runnymede. Justice Denham established in 1624 a foundation to house five poor widows, aged 50 years or over and having strong local connections. 'No cursers, blasphemers, nor drunkards, no idle persons, no gadders abroad, no wanderers about from house to house, no tale bearers or busy bodies' need apply.

P1795

P1905

THE DENHAM ALMSHOUSES *Egham Hill   c.1905*

The original buildings were established at the foot of Egham Hill, the opposite end of the town from Denham's mansion. In about 1764 'being ruinous and prone to decay' they were rebuilt. The site had been large enough for each almswoman to have her own garden but in 1815 the Trustees let some of the garden land to increase the Trust's income, it having been under-endowed. In 1859 a police station was built on a portion of garden land, the architect being Charles Henry Howell. At the end of the century more land was leased to Surrey County Council for the building of a Technical Institute and to William and Edwin Oldridge to build a forge and two villas. First the Police Station and Technical Institute and later the Denham Almshouses were demolished in the widening of Egham Hill in the early 1970s. The lady pictured in the doorway of the almshouses may well have been Louisa Poole who was matron and almswoman between 1904 and 1917.

DENHAM HOUSE *towards the east end of the High Street c.1937*

This house was demolished in 1937 and the present Police Station built on the site. Denham House had been built in the grounds of Sir John Denham's 17th century mansion, 'The Place'. The building in the photograph was owned and occupied in the last 20 years of the 19th century and up to about 1923 by the medical practioner Henry E. Giffard and his family. Subsequently the house, garden, stabling and paddock were owned briefly by Dr Campbell Ford before the premises were taken over by Surrey County Council. The road by this time had changed to meet the growing demands of the motorist: widened, asphalted, well-lit and sign-posted. Beyond can be seen The Avenue with the sign of the White Lion.

P1457

STRODE'S SCHOOL AND ALMSHOUSES
High Street rebuilt 1828-39

Another Egham benefactor was Henry Strode. By his will of 1703 he bequeathed £6,000 for the building of a school house for the education of the poor children of Egham together with almshouses for the elderly. One of the Trustees for this charity was the Worshipful Company of Coopers of London of which Henry Strode was a member. The photograph shows the second school building consisting of a central chapel, master's house and school room. This, with the almshouses at right-angles to the west of the school, was put in hand by architect George Smith with builder Richard Dean in 1828. The architecture was Gothic with mellow red brick and string coursing under a slate roof. The block of almshouses to the east was not built until 1839. The almshouses were converted to other uses in 1911 and the alms people moved out. The foundation stone for a new school on the same site was laid in 1915 and it opened as a boys' grammar school in 1919. The school became a sixth-form college in 1975.

The Almshouses, Egham.

P28

STROUD, CANNELL and CO, COACH BUILDERS *c.1862*

This is an early photograph of 1 and 2 High Street. James Stroud himself, pictured on the left, was born in Trowbridge, Wiltshire, and established the Egham business in 1862. He specialised in making all forms of light vehicles to order, including waggonettes and phaetons. He also carried out repairs and painting 'at reasonable prices'. As a master craftsman he was entitled to instruct apprentices in his art. Such a one in 1866 was William Strangeman, a fourteen-year-old, born in Camberwell and bound to Mr Stroud for seven years in the sum of £50, met by the boy's uncle. As well as his board and lodging, washing, mending and medical expenses, the apprentice was to receive 3d per week, rising to 2s 6d (12½p) in his final year. William was still lodging with James Stroud and his little family in 1871, so he must have served his master faithfully as required. By the turn of the century the firm of James Stroud had moved to Station Road and Jesse Cooper and Son, also coach builders, had taken over the High Street premises. In the 1920s the Egham Motor Co was installed in number 2 and in the 1930s the building was demolished in the construction of the Egham bypass.

P87

THE KING'S ARMS *c.1950*

There has been an inn on this site, the junction of High Street with the present Langham Place, at least since the 17th century. In the early 18th century it was owned and run by Thomas and then by John Bristow, until it passed by marriage to a branch of the Oades family. Later it became a tied house of Neville Reid and Co, brewers of Windsor. It is one of Egham's Grade II listed buildings. The cottage next door, once a wheelwright's shop and shown here covered in creeper, is also listed. Now La Bonne Franquette Restaurant, it was popular as The Old House Café and Tea Gardens in the earlier part of the century. The King's Arms has, in 1988, been taken over by La Bonne Franquette and re-opened as a café and bar called 'Next Door'.

P558A

BOSHER, CORN and COAL MERCHANTS   *c.1893*

These premises were at 8 and 9 High Street. The grass in the foreground is a reminder of the still rural nature of Egham at that time. John Bosher owned not only the house, shop and granary shown but stabling and even meadow land in the High Street. He also owned a 75 acre farm in Stroude that gave him the right of killing game. He also rented pasture at Great Fosters, Runnymede and Kingswood. The erstwhile Bosher family home, the centre building in the picture, was demolished in 1986. Readers will remember it as C. and T. Radio, 'Ron Clarke's wireless shop'.

P694

HIGH STREET   *looking west   c.1910*

Earlier this century the west end of the High Street was a significant focus of trading. Janes' Emporium, Egham's own department store, shown in the foreground, was the chief reason for this. It sold all forms of clothing, linoleum, carpets and linen. Thomas Janes, the founder of the Emporium, began business in Egham in 1863 when he rented Wellclose House from Alexander Oades, eventually taking over the whole site, together with the freehold. In 1938 Janes and Sons ceased trading. During the Second World War the building was used as a British Restaurant, one of the extremely cheap, one shilling (5p) a head, establishments provided by the local authority. The building was demolished in the early 1960s to make way for the Public Library and new Egham Urban District Council Offices opened in 1963. The Council Offices themselves became surplus to requirements when Egham merged with Chertsey in 1974 to become the Runnymede District. Runnymede was incorporated as a Borough in 1978 and the Egham Council Offices demolished early in 1986. Sheltered housing was built on the site. Janes provided gowns for the patients at Holloway Sanatorium, and Miss Hawkins, chief cutter and fitter, walked the three miles or so from Egham to Virginia Water carrying suitcases full of dresses. Once she had entered a room for a fitting with a patient, the door was always locked behind her.

P481

COOMBES' TOY SHOP *1930s*

This shop, opposite Walnut Tree Gardens, was demolished with other properties in the same block in 1986 for office development.
Mr George H. Coombes, the shopkeeper is seen here with his wife, in the doorway of their toyshop. They rented the house, shop, buildings and garden at number 26 in the 1920s and 1930s. The family came originally from east London. 'Winner' was a popular record label of the time, its motif being a race horse.

HIGH STREET *looking west c.1905*

Janes' shop is glimpsed distantly on the right-hand side, while the garden of Walnut Tree Cottage fills the background on the left. The well-displayed basket shop on the left was kept by the basket-maker and cooper, Edward G. Nash in the early years of the 20th century. The building with the arcaded windows included Chilvers' the butcher's shop and Fensom's the plumber's. The west half was demolished in 1973 and the remaining part by 1986. A large office block was built on the site. On the right is Box and Gilham's the stationery firm, which acted as a special depot for toys and dolls. They also sold electro-plate and silver goods, Goss china and postcards as well as stationery items. It was Box and Gilham who published Frederick Turner's *Egham, a History of the Parish Under Church and Crown* in 1926. This book, the standard history of the old parish, was limited to an edition of 250 copies and sold at one guinea (105p). Strode's School wall is on the immediate right.

High Street, Egham.

P480

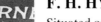

F. H. HYDE'S LEATHER SHOP   *c.1914*

Situated opposite Strode's College this was a familiar sight in Egham until recently. The shop window had not been modified over the years and the customer still steps down into the shop. This indicates the age of the building as the highway has been built up over the years. The photograph shows the proprietor himself with his then small son, Ronald, who later took over the business. An advertisement in the *Egham Directory* for 1914 describes Mr Hyde as 'Sadler and Harness Maker'. Portmanteaus and travelling trunks were repaired and light and heavy harness made on the premises. All stable requisites were kept in stock at that time. For a short time before Mr Hyde took over in 1911, a plumber had operated his business from the shop, while fish was also sold there. This was only a brief interruption, however, for the previous occupant, William Trumper and before him his father, Arthur, had also been sadlers, providing Egham with leather goods, from the 1840s until about 1909.

P238A

HIGH STREET   *looking east   c.1916*

On the right are the premises of W. V. King, builder and decorator. Just visible on the left is J. & W. Gilbert's, stationers and booksellers. This photograph is one of their own postcards. Next door is H. W. Herbert's pharmacy. Mr Herbert provided an invaluable service to the people of Egham. He was not only a family chemist but extracted teeth and fitted dentures, supplied spectacles, photographic and horticultural chemicals and surgical appliances as well as the expected patent medicines and toiletries. He stocked mineral waters in silver-plated syphons as well as veterinary preparations. Mr Herbert was a member of the Pharmaceutical Society and dispensed all medicines personally. An office of Cross and Herbert Ltd, the pharmaceutical group, remains at 41 High Street, while the retail shop is now situated in The Precinct. Further on is the gabled roof and shop blind of Egham's other department store, H. Weller's.

H. WELLER'S *1911*

Here 'the oldest drapery establishment in town' is in celebratory mood for the Coronation of HM King George V and HM Queen Mary. Weller's was said to have been the best decorated shop in town on that occasion. It sold carpets and linoleum, boots and shoes as well as ladies' and gentlemen's outfits. The beautiful staircase was a striking feature. The premises, 42-4 High Street, were designed as one building between 1823-24 for Gilbert Elstone, draper. He paid one shilling (5p) yearly to the Cooper's Company for the privilege of retaining his windows on the west side of his property that overlooked Strode's School land. The firm of Weller took over the premises in the 1850s and stayed until 1921. There were opportunities for young ladies of Egham to become apprentice dressmakers and young men draper's assistants.

P118A

BUDGEN'S GROCERY STORE *c.1905*

Next door to Weller's was Budgen's grocery shop, the staff here proudly displaying their wares. In the late 1840s, young Edward Budgen left his father's grocery shop in Reigate and set up his own establishment in Egham. Soon he was employing four men, including his younger brother, Frederick, then eight men and a boy. As the business prospered, other branches were opened in the family name. The provision store continued to do well throughout the 19th century, a younger Edward taking over from his father in Egham in due course. Edward Budgen, junior, was most active in local affairs, serving on the Parish Council and acting as Chairman of the Egham Schools' managers in the early part of this century. The business was sold in about 1920 to Alfred Button, a food wholesale company, though the Budgen name was retained. Thus began the expansion that led to today's chain of supermarkets. The Egham branch closed in 1965 and the building was refitted as two retail shops.

P216A

DRAKE and MOUNT LTD *c.1910*

This site, on the corner of High Street and Station Road included in the mid-19th century a granary, shed and yards. A chimney and engine-house were added later. The corn and seed business was carried out there by first Henry and then William Paice. William proudly displayed the royal standard as he was corn and seed merchant 'by royal warrant to Her Majesty (Queen Victoria) and the Prince of Wales (later HM King Edward VII)'. Mill stones associated with William Paice survive in the grounds of Friends' Meeting House in Limes Road. The original siting of the mill stones is not known. William Paice himself lived in a house called The Limes situated in the High Street where the Egham Youth Centre now stands. A steam engine installed at the Station Road corn merchant's premises for which a tall chimney was necessary was dismantled in 1948. The chimney itself was demolished shortly afterwards. The corn merchants also had their own 400yd railway track, the waggons horse-drawn. It ran from Egham Station, across School Lane and Church Road, through the orchard, where the Post Office now stands, to the works. In the early 20th century Drake and Mount, who had coal and corn depots at Sunningdale and Virginia Water Stations, took over the business. The building was demolished in 1960-61 and a supermarket and shops built on the site.

P1112B

STATION ROAD *c.1906*

In the right foreground is the Prince of Wales once a Meux's house and built on an old gravel pit site. Described as a lodging house in 1892 it catered for a 'low class of people'. It was demolished in the late 1970s to make way for the Egham ring road, but its inn sign may still be seen in The Egham Museum. The low building next to it was a barber's shop as the long striped pole indicates. The solidly-built Railway Hotel was designed to accommodate travellers on the new fangled iron horse. The hotel owners, Friary Holroyd of Guildford supported 'a respectable bar trade'. The population more than doubled between the 1850s and the 1890s and more houses and shops were built in Station Road, once the rural Rusham Green Road. A small fair, with double roundabouts was sometimes held on the orchard ground on the left. Cory Brothers later had an oil storage depot roughly where the young lady cyclists are. This was removed in the 1960s.

P689A

EGHAM STATION   *c.1970*

The Staines, Wokingham & Woking Junction Railway opened to Ascot (including Egham) on 4 June 1856. It was an independent railway operated by the London & South Western Railway (LSWR). On 25 March 1858 it was leased to the LSWR who later bought it outright. It ran from Staines (later Staines Junction and still later Staines Central) on the Windsor line of the LSWR, which had been completed in 1848, to Wokingham on the South Eastern Railway. Locomotives used included the Adams '415' class (4-4-2 tank locomotives) and in particular the Drummond 'M7' class (0-4-4). These operated the line until electrification came in 1939. The Weybridge line was electrified on 3 January 1937. The LSWR had completed a spur from their main line at Weybridge to Chertsey in 1848 and this was extended to Virginia Water to a junction with the Wokingham line in 1866. Egham station, built in the 1850s by Oades & Son, was rebuilt in 1984.

P819

'F1 JUMBO' ENGINE No 1195   *in Egham Station*   *1937-38*

This picture shows not an 'M7' engine but an 'F1 Jumbo', originally used by the South Eastern Railway and rebuilt by Wainwright. Several were tried by the Southern, the successors to the LSWR on the Reading route. Judging by the presence of the roof brackets for destination boards, the coaches shown are down-graded main line corridor stock. This would be among the last steam passenger trains on the Reading service. Electrification brought faster and more frequent services. In 1909, on weekdays the first train to Waterloo was the 7.48am from Egham which took 42min and stopped at Staines, Richmond and Vauxhall. The Vauxhall stop was for the collection of tickets. In addition there was a train about every two hours from Woking to Windsor calling at Egham and 'Staines High Street'. This latter station was sited where the Windsor line bridge crosses Staines High Street.

STATION ROAD SCHOOLS   *c.1910*

These were the Egham Board Schools and catered for boys, girls and infants separately. They were built in 1868 out of the Poor's Allotment Fund on Crown land gifted by HM Queen Victoria. The architect was Charles Henry Howell, at that time County Surveyor for Surrey and the builder was A. L. Oades of Egham. In 1875 the average attendance at the school was 171 pupils; by 1894 it had increased to 387. As the Manor School, it closed in 1975, was eventually demolished and a housing estate built on its site. The school bells survive, refurbished by the Parents' Association. One is on permanent loan to The Egham Museum and the other on display in Manorcroft County First and Middle School on the southern side of the railway line.

In the second, somewhat later photograph, the children are celebrating a patriotic occasion, possibly Empire Day.

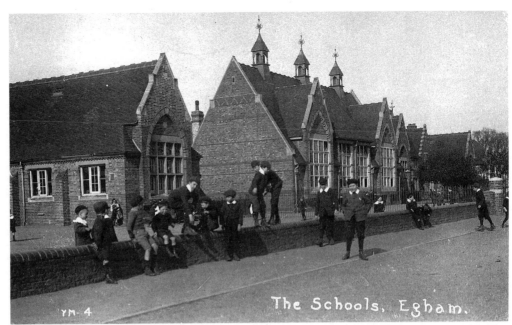

P728A

ST ANN'S HEATH SCHOOL   *1930s*

Here the children are celebrating a patriotic occasion, possibly Empire Day.

P728

MILTON PARK   *1865*

The Manor of Milton (or Myddleton) was mentioned as early as the middle of the 12th century. Indeed, the Middleton family itself held it for more than 400 years. In 1519 it was purchased by Richard Fox, the founder of Corpus Christi College, Oxford and leased to the Moore family for over two centuries. From the Moores it passed to first the Edgell family and then in 1781 to Richard Wyatt, by virtue of his marriage. His artistic taste and beautiful daughters made the house a cultural and social centre. His son, Edgell Wyatt Edgell pulled down the old mansion and rebuilt it in Georgian style. Between 1864 and 1872 the whole of the Manor was acquired from Corpus Christi College by the Baron de Worms, who enlarged both the park and the mansion in 1887. In 1948 it was purchased by the British Leather Manfacturers' Research Association. Johnson Wax Ltd bought the house and some 12 acres of land 30 years later and have restored many of its former beauties while operating it as a modern research centre.

   The second photograph shows a family group at Milton Park in 1886.

P1247A

THORPE LEA HOUSE   *c.1900*

In 1794 Sir Edward Blackett of Matfen, Northumberland bought, for £950, Thorpe Lea House, a property situated at the corner of Vicarage Road and Thorpe Lea Road, from Ann, the widow of Thomas Johnstone, a Staines draper. Sir Edward stayed only a few years, selling to James Ludovic Grant for £1,500 in 1802. It remained a private house until the Second World War when it was requisitioned by the War Office. After the war, it returned to private hands but later had a chequered career as a cheap boarding house. A fire subsequently destroyed most of the original features but the property was rebuilt in its old style and is now a business headquarters. The photograph shows a group on the lawns at the back of the house.

P711A

P959

P2787

GREAT FOSTERS *c.1900*

Great Fosters, a gabled mansion of brick and stone, with chalk-mullioned windows, was stated by Frederick Turner to be 'by far the finest relic of antiquity in the parish'. Despite the date 1598 sculptured over the doorway, Turner was of the opinion that the present house was built at the beginning of the 17th century, probably by Sir Antony Mayne. Like any building of such age there are many legends associated with it. In the old dining-room the plaster ceilings are decorated with devices used by Anne Boleyn and her daughter, Queen Elizabeth. In the old drawing-room above are various badges of the Percies of Northumberland. The next owner, Sir John Doderidge, a judge and member of the Society of Antiquaries, was probably responsible for the sun-dial in the garden and the Armillary sphere inside the house. Another judge, Sir Robert Foster, later Lord Chief Justice, lived there during the Civil War. As a staunch Royalist he followed King Charles I's retreat to Oxford, leaving his wife to cope with five children, twelve servants and numerous visitations from Parliamentary troops in search of billets, food and horses. It is often thought that Sir Robert gave his name to the mansion, but 'lands on the west called Fosters' were mentioned in the court rolls of Thorpe in 1521.

THE HALKETT FAMILY AT GREAT FOSTERS *c.1900*

In the 18th and early 19th centuries the house was kept as a private lunatic asylum, latterly by Dr George Frederick Furnival, a respected Egham physician. Great Fosters had suffered from a multiplicity of owners; no family had held it for more than two generations. In the 1860s, however, it was acquired by Colonel Halkett, a Baron of the Kingdom of Hanover, who spent a great deal of money restoring the place. Perhaps it was he who chose to tease the historian with strange devices. The photograph shows a family group at the door of their home and includes William James Halkett and the Misses Halkett. The Baroness herself, who lived at Great Fosters for nearly 50 years, was of Danish origin and a friend of HM Queen Alexandra, herself a Danish princess. In 1910 the mansion again lay derelict and was once more rescued, this time by the Hon G. S. Montague, who had the task not only of restoring, but of rebuilding the neglected fabric. Today antiquity combines with modern hotel and conference facilities.

P861

P859A

THORPE LEE HOUSE   *c.1900*

Thorpe Lee House has disappeared under the M25. Sir Edward Blackett built it as his new house in 1802. He died in 1804 and is buried in Ripon Cathedral. The house, the entrance for which was in Clockhouse Lane, became for a time, the home of his son William the 5th Baronet. One of Sir William's sons, John Charles Blackett, who was born at Thorpe, entered the Royal Navy and was one of the last cadets to be trained on HMS *Victory*. He lived at Thorpe Lee House until he died in 1896. His daughter remained in residence. In the 1930s the house was an hotel owned by Mountcombe Hotels Ltd. Like the Blackett's old house, it too was requisitioned by the War Office in the Second World War. The photograph shows the house in its grand days when Miss Blackett was in residence.

P507

THE EGHAM VOLUNTARY FIRE BRIGADE   *c.1884*

The Brigade was formed in November 1884, formalising the somewhat *ad hoc* arrangements that had been in force since 1827. It is probable that the photograph commemorates their first drill. The new engine, proudly displayed on Daisy Meadow, Vicarage Road, had cost £200 which had been raised by public subscription. It was drawn by two horses that had to be rounded up before use with the engine. The Brigade Captain, W. J. Simpson, is shown in the centre of the picture. All Brigade members were volunteers who would have to leave their full-time work to attend fires. The charges were met by those who called on their services. In 1913 Egham received its first motor fire engine, *The Phoenix*, generously presented to the town by Baron Bruno Schröder. The Brigade remained in being until about 1938 when the National Fire Service was formed.

High Street, Egham.

HIGH STREET   *looking west   c.1906*

The Crown inn sign, Weller's emporium and Budgen's grocery shop can be seen in the distance. On the left, outside the yellow-bricked Georgian house called Aubrey Haw, is a lantern, advertising 'dentist'. The dentist occupying the house in the 1920s was Reginald S. Topple, 'a dapper, spat-wearing gentleman'. On the north side, next to the grocer's shop and indeed owned by Edward Budgen, is the Old Bank, now Barclays Bank, but then rented to Thomas Ashby & Co. Ashby's Bank was established in 1796 and came to Egham in 1866. Thirty years later this branch was re-built in its present style. Between the Old Bank and the London and Provincial Bank were premises owned and occupied in the second half of the 19th century by Robert Oades. His daughter, Mary Ann, lived there well into this century. Robert was an auctioneer, surveyor and land and estate agent in the High Street. Just visible in the right foreground is a corner of the garden of Dr William T. Drew's house, Littlecroft.

P36

DAVID GREIG'S GROCERY STORE, AND ELECTRICITY SHOW ROOMS   *c.1950*

When the house became vacant in the late 1920s, shop fronts were added and the Electricity Co and David Greig's grocery chain opened branches there. For many years the garden remained as a recreation area for electricity workers, the little summer-house becoming a pavilion. In 1988 it has all disappeared to make way for more office building.

P2213A

P975A

HIGH STREET *looking east c.1912*

Opposite was Egham's first cinema, The Gem. The parade of shops next to it was built in about 1908 and still survives. The Greenfield family of ironmongers and china sellers were among the first to move in. 'The Old Iron Pot' hanging from the gable advertises their wares. All the shops were owned at that time by Mr Francis Powell. He was also a partner in The Electric Supply Syndicate which had been established on the same site in 1906. Thus it was that the shops in this part of the High Street were the first to enjoy the convenience of electric light. Indeed on the right of the cinema entrance can be seen a transformer kiosk of a type made for the British Electric Transformer Co in about 1910. Only one example remains in this area: outside a house adjoining the old Co-op in Thorpe.

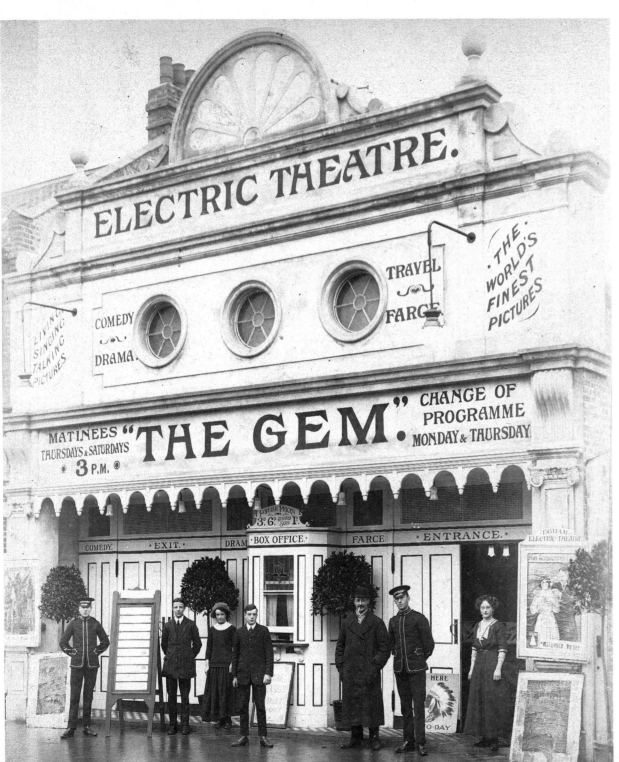

THE GEM CINEMA *opened 1910*

In 1910 Mr Powell built his 'Electric Theatre' between Aubrey Haw and the new shops. Being a diamond cutter, he gave the cinema the unusual name of The Gem after his craft. At the time of the Grand Opening Mr Cecil Court was the manager. Reserved seats cost 1s (5p), stalls 6d (2½p) and unreserved seats 3d (1½p). The audience sat on hard bench seats beneath a domed ceiling, decorated with little cherubs set in illuminated glass panels. By the time talking films were introduced in 1928 The Gem had a rival, the Bohemia, a little further east along the High Street. Both cinemas were run at that time by Mr Sidney Stotesbury, but the Bohemia, later the Savoy, was one of the first houses to introduce the new 'talking machines'. The Gem closed soon afterwards. In the Second World War the building was used for military purposes, whilst, postwar, the firm of Kar Sales always had a vast selection of second-hand motors on display there. Prior to its demolition in 1981, a section of scaffolding around the building collapsed into the High Street. Fortunately no one was injured.

P385

HIGH STREET *looking east* 1904

The gabled building on the right was Egham's Post Office, later used as the offices of the Urban District Council. William H. Gardner was the Sub-Postmaster. A Royal Mail Daimler motor van stands near the garage. Next to the Post Office can be seen Cotswold House, the residence of William Wadham Floyer, one of Egham's surgeons and medical officers. Outside is a boy pushing a milk churn on a hand-cart. In the 18th and 19th centuries the 'Carriage Road — Egham Street' as it appears on some old plans, contained several such highly desirable residences. One survivor is the present Constitutional Club. Once it was the home of the respected Egham blacksmith, Richard Gates. The building still carries a Sun Insurance firemark and from its policy of 1796 we know what household possession he insured. On the left is Thomas Rayment's music and fancy goods shop. Mr Rayment had an unusual further qualification: he taught Esperanto.

P215A

DRAKE'S MOTOR & CYCLE DEPOT *c.1904*

Egham took to the horseless carriage with enthusiasm. Early in the century John Drake turned an erstwhile builder's workshop into one of Egham's first motor garages. It would, however, be a long time before horse-drawn vehicles disappeared completely from the High Street. Later the garage was taken over by the Egham Motor Co, who subsequently moved to the western end of the High Street. The premises reopened as Vincent's Radio and Cycle Shop in 1932. One of the older High Street properties with wells in both kitchen and garden, it became the site of Tesco's supermarket in the 1960s.

P976A

THE NAGS HEAD INN   *c.1901*

Next door to Rayment's was this inn, the name of which appeared in the Egham Parish Register in 1689 and also in 18th century directories. In the 19th century it was owned by Farnell & Co, brewers of Isleworth. In 1915 its licence was not renewed and the premises were taken over by Turner & Sons, Fishmongers. In the 1970s it was used as a veterinary hospital. The inn name survives in a mosaic in the doorway. The buildings in this block are part of the White House development scheme, which has retained much of the original façades.

P369A

HERD BROTHERS CYCLE WORKS   *c.1910*

Further east along the High Street, on the present site of Woolworth's were once to be seen the fascinating windows of Edwin and Cecil Herd's cycle shop. Note the gas lamp, and the cycle wheel that advertises the wares. As well as building cycles to order, the brothers sold paraffin, bee-hives, gramophones and records and repaired 'talking machines'. To a small boy the shop was a veritable treasure trove, especially as gliders fired by catapults were to be obtained there. Leaning against the shop is a motorised bicycle. These had all but disappeared by the end of the 1930s but new versions appeared after the Second World War. The Herd family had traded in Egham since 1840, first as boot and shoe makers, and then as cycle agents. Mr 'Ned' Herd is seen in the photograph outside the shop. He traded until about 1949, then for a while china was sold there until in 1955 F. W. Woolworth Ltd bought the site.

P886A

ELECTION CAMPAIGN *1910*

This is Miss Kathleen Jackson of Claremont, Egham, campaigning for Mr Donald Macmaster, the successful Conservative and Liberal Unionist candidate. Her bicycle and that of her young companion were decked out with Unionist favours. She was described by the new MP himself as 'picturesque and graceful' and even better 'in action on the date of polling, with the colours flying to the breeze arranged in such an artistic style'. There were jubilant scenes in Egham when the result was known. A torchlight procession, headed by the Town Band paraded through the principal streets and the Constitutional Club was illuminated by coloured fire. The Egham Liberal Club, not to be outdone, put up this notice in its window: 'Macmaster majority 4,613. Good luck to him. Are we downhearted? No!'. Donald Macmaster, King's Counsel and later Baronet, was born in Canada in 1846. He remained the MP for the Chertsey Division from 1910 until his death in 1922. He is buried in Virginia Water Churchyard, having resided at Merlewood on Callow Hill.

P703A

JOHN DRAKE & CO *c.1908*

John Drake took over this shop early in the 20th century and it remained a feature of Egham High Street for almost 50 years. He employed plumbers, smiths and sheet metal workers and was able to install electric light, telephones and heating systems as well as supplying tools for all trades. Previously the shop had been owned and occupied by W. H. Gardener whose family had been Egham smiths and ironmongers since the beginning of the 19th century. Mr Gardener's initials and the date of the rebuilding, 1877, are to be seen in the stonework beside the upper windows. As the Sub-Registrar for Births and Deaths, Mr Gardener offered his office and his services in the establishment of a labour registry in Egham in 1885. It was the brainchild of Nathaniel Louis Cohen of Round Oak, Englefield Green and became the first successful public labour registry in the country. Many people in Egham were literally on the bread line at the time, for the building of Royal Holloway College and Holloway Sanatorium was virtually complete, leaving a large number of workmen unemployed. The Registry served Egham for nearly ten years, Nathaniel Cohen, an active man in local affairs, being ahead of his time in political thought. The Labour Exchange Act did not pass into law until 1909.

P3077

P1057A

C. A. BLACKLOCK, FLORIST, FRUITERER and SEEDSMAN *c.1926*

The proprietor is seen here delivering in the district, his horse and cart loaded with goods.

64 HIGH STREET *1920s*

Mr Blacklock traded from his shop at 64 High Street next door to Clarke's the butchers. He ran the business from 1912 until 1931. In 1841 the premises were listed as James Dodd's crockery shop, but in the latter part of the 19th century it became a green grocer's shop, the proprietor being Walter James Feltham. It will be remembered as Jack Greaves' electrical repair shop, which was demolished early in 1974.

P3078

J. HOPKINS & SON, BAKERS and CONFECTIONERS *c.1901*

Next door to the Hop Blossom beer house, this was the family's second shop in the High Street, the other one being at number 11. Joseph Hopkins came to Egham from Middlesex in about 1861, having just completed his apprenticeship, and settled down to establish a long-lasting family tradition. By 1881 he had eight children, and, as if that was not enough, added two young journeymen bakers and three lodgers to his household. Fortunately for his wife, Elinor, two young girls also lived in to help look after this extended family. Joshua Lawrence Hopkins, Joseph's eighth child, took over the business when his father retired. This second shop, 67 High Street, may be better remembered as The Penny Stores or the Bazaar around the time of the Great War. In the 1960s an old bakehouse was recorded at the back of the premises.

P559A

HIGH STREET *looking west* c.1920

On the left can be seen the greenhouses belonging to W. F. Parsons' Nursery. A Fellow of the Royal Horticultural Society and specialist in fruit trees, roses and herbaceous plants, he used land at Thorpe Lea for horticultural purposes. He was also a landscape gardener, provided decorative plants for special occasions and made up bouquets and wreaths. During Ascot Week Mr Parsons used to decorate his sign with roses and the pavement outside with tall fuchsias. He was privileged to decorate the Royal Stand at Ascot Race Course. Two family houses lie back behind the trees. Then can be seen another view of the King's Head inn. Their cellars which ran together were thought by some members of the Parsons family to be haunted. Jutting out on the right-hand side is Victor Badois' electrical shop. The comparatively low white building on the right was at that time John Pook's the hairdressers. It appears in the water colour view of Egham High Street painted by John Hassell in 1820, now on show in The Egham Museum. On the immediate right is Mrs Clara Douglas's baker's and confectioner's shop.

P1141A

THE INTERNATIONAL TEA CO LTD c.1913

This general grocer's was retailing at the eastern end of the High Street, numbers 87 and 88, for more than 70 years. Indeed, at the turn of the century it must have been one of the first businesses to move into the building that had previously been the Catherine Wheel's annexe. Celindo tea seemed to have been the current shop window promotion.

HIGH STREET *in flood* 1894

Immediately in the right foreground are the houses known as King's Row. Among the oldest buildings at this end of the High Street they remain substantially unaltered except for shop-front extensions, which include, in 1988, the Chinese Take-away at number 95 on the corner of Denham road. This house was formerly the home of Edward Simmons, a Relieving Officer for the Windsor Union, and later his son Arthur, the bearded figure fourth from the left with his wife, Susan. Further on the right with a tall archway for coaches and a hanging sign is the Catherine Wheel hotel, forerunner of the present building. Directly opposite the hotel are houses, and behind the trees farm property, all since absorbed by building. The 1894 flood level, recorded at Bell Weir lock-keeper's cottage, reached 14in above the towing path.

P2264

P3079

Egham Floods. 1904

A 1660

P349

THE AVENUE IN FLOOD   *1904*

There was always the danger of flooding in winter and travellers from Old Windsor were warned not to attempt the Windsor Road route to Egham when the river was running high. A finger post sign opposite the Bells of Ouseley still refers to the distance to Egham as being 2½ miles 'except at highwater'.

EGHAM IN FLOOD   *1915*

In this photograph the sightseers are looking across the flooded meadows from where the Glanty Roundabout now stands, towards the Angler's Rest hotel on the right. The Windsor Road is to their left and the flooded sign post points towards The Causeway.

P542A

THE GLANTY ROUNDABOUT IN FLOOD   *1947*

The 1947 flood was the worst since 1894, the water level rising 8½in above the towing path. Hedgerows in Windsor Road were completely submerged; a gold fish was caught in Wendover Road and the Paripan paint factory became an island. A Paripan employee of the time recalls with pleasure the company's celebrated advertisement, 'The more you wash it the better it looks', being particularly appropriate to the paint factory being surrounded with water. People had to be rescued by army DUKWs or by inflatable dinghy from the low-lying areas. Despite the water lapping round the posts, the gas lights on the Glanty Roundabout remained alight. The debris hung about the hedgerows for nearly a year after the event. The Glanty Hotel, demolished in the early 1970s, is in the background. In the centre a London Transport central area ST type motor bus, number 117, Egham to Hounslow, is splashing past the roundabout.

P2423

The Avenue, Egham

THE AVENUE *looking east c.1908*

The fine building on the right was known as Forge House, a typical late 18th century gentleman's residence. In 1871 Edwyn Allum Esq, lived there. A man of private means he was obviously progressive in his views on education, for both his son, Charles, and his daughter, Clare, were students at Cambridge University. In the 1930s it gloried in the name of 'Cliff's Wonder Bar', after its proprietor, Edward Clifford Huet. Alongside the cafe were a petrol station, car park and garage. After its demolition in 1940, two semi-detached houses were built on the site. These are, in 1988, being replaced by retirement homes. On the left can be seen the white building that housed Westcot Ltd's offices, demolished in 1979. The factory, manufacturing heavy overalls and later also jeans, lay back on the site now occupied by the head office and servicing works of Messrs Ketts, Radio, TV and Domestic Appliances. The Victoria inn can be seen in the distance.

P26A

THE VICTORIA INN *The Avenue c.1908*

The small, square, white building with a veranda was built in the early years of HM Queen Victoria's reign. The inn was reconstructed in 1936. The people of Egham, or the travellers on the road must have been a thirsty lot, for there were already the White Lion, 150 yard west, the Coach and Horses 100 yard east, not to mention the Nelson beer house opposite. The Victoria catered for the 'working class and beanfeasters'. John W. Tow came to the Victoria at the beginning of the 20th century, obviously determined to make a success of his new venture. He remained at this Ashby's inn for nearly 30 years.

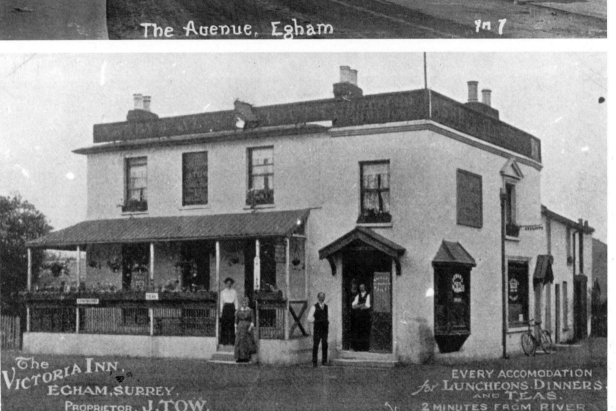

The VICTORIA INN, EGHAM, SURREY, PROPRIETOR, J. TOW.

EVERY ACCOMODATION for LUNCHEONS DINNERS AND TEAS. 2 MINUTES FROM RIVER

P244A

THE GLANTY *1908*

This old name means the landing place frequented by hawks or kites. It first appears in a medieval version of a Saxon chronicle describing the bounds of Egham and Thorpe. The Glanty cottages and the sign of the Coach and Horses can be seen in the distance. Both inns welcomed cyclists and served teas.

P1109B

THE COACH AND HORSES INN *1971*

The existence of trade tokens shows that there was a Coach and Horses inn on this site in the 17th century. It was owned in the 19th century by the Hall and de Egville families, James Herret de Egville being a hop merchant of Worcester. Cannings, the brewers of Windsor, leased the inn in 1914 and Hodgsons, the Kingston brewery company, bought it in 1925 for £3,500. It was demolished in 1974 to make way for the Egham section of the M25, opened in 1977. An eight-day wall clock and a right-of-way sign are preserved in The Egham Museum. Near the inn sign was an early 19th century cast-iron water pump constructed for the Bedfont-Bagshot Turnpike Co to dampen the dusty coach road. It was saved by Egham-by-Runnymede Historical Society and with the co-operation of Runnymede Borough Council resited in Walnut Tree Gardens in 1981.

P1685

NOS 27, 28 and 29 THE AVENUE   c.1935

Before the Egham bypass was built these cottages were to be seen at the junction of The Avenue with the Lower Windsor Road. Adjoining on The Avenue side and indeed built on part of the cottages' gardens was The Avenue Motor Co or Tee's Garage, as it was more usually called, after its owner, Edward Tee. The cottages originally consisted of one house, with a large warehouse, stables and loft at the Windsor Road end. Like all the properties in this area the gardens, and even the kitchens, which were lower than the living rooms, were liable to flood. On The Avenue side of the building was a public fire alarm push button. The occupier was paid a small annual fee for allowing the installation of batteries in one of the bedrooms. These furnished current to operate the alarm at Egham Fire Station. On The Causeway bank can be seen the premises of Mr Brooks, well known as a second-hand cycle dealer. Opposite is the inn sign of the Coach and Horses. The construction of the Egham bypass can be seen, encroaching on the cottages, a grim foreshadowing of the present vista of roundabout and motorway fly-over.

P502

COFFEE STALL   *Glanty Bank   c.1935*

This stall stood right in the path of the Egham bypass. It was popular with men on their way to work and doubtless equally well patronised by the road builders, with tea and coffee at 1d (½p) or 2d (1p) a cup. The footpath, along which cycling was prohibited on pain of a fine of 40s (£2), went down to Strode's field and indeed is the present route of the bypass from the Glanty Roundabout. The bill boards show that at the Majestic Cinema, Staines, a double bill featured Constance Bennett in 'Sealed Lips', supported by Joel McCrea in 'Chance at Heaven' made in 1933. Billy Reid and Queenie May were appearing as top of the bill at the Chiswick Empire. The Kensitas Cigarette Co was giving away 'Flags of the Empire' with its products.

P1466

P1444

THE CAUSEWAY *looking towards Egham c.1907*

The Causeway was constructed in the 13th century on the initiative of the wool merchant, Thomas de Oxenford, who wished his pack horses to use the road from Staines Bridge in all weathers. Before that travellers and goods had to detour through Chertsey when flood water submerged Egham's lower levels. Throughout the centuries there were quarrels between Egham and Staines about who was responsible for its maintenance, a problem not resolved until the roadway was taken over by the County in 1869. Attempts by Egham-by-Runnymede Historical Society in 1987 to get The Causeway declared an ancient monument were unsuccessful. Along The Causeway was Woodhaw, a large mansion built on the site of the ancient landing-place of Wodehaghe. In the first half of the 19th century the famous 'Old Brown Windsor Soap' was made there by the Paris family of soap manufacturers. The soap factory and a wharf were included in the estate. Prior to its demolition, just before the Second World War, Woodhaw was an hotel. An estate of the same name was built on the site. The old lodge remains. It will be remembered as kennels.

THE LAGONDA MOTORS *The Causeway c.1935*

The motor company was founded by Wilbur Adam Gunn, an American sewing machine engineer who came to this country at the end of the 19th century. In a few years he had set up a motor-cycle factory in the grounds of his house in Thorpe Road. He named his company Lagonda after the Red Indian name, meaning Buck's Horns, of the creek in western Ohio where the Gunn family had settled in the early 19th century. From manufacturing motor-cycles he moved to tricars and then to cars and as the demand grew extended the works north along Thorpe Road and into The Causeway. For a while the Ship Inn, popular with race-goers and beanfeasters, was almost surrounded by the motor company. It is said that there were doors conveniently placed at the back of the hostelry for Lagonda workers to use out of hours. The further extension of the factory in 1935 coincided with Surrey County Council's plans to widen The Causeway. In 1936 the small Georgian inn was demolished and rebuilt on the opposite side of the road. When the Lagonda company merged with Aston Martin in 1947 the factory site was sold to Petters Ltd, Engine Manufacturers.

P1420

LOOKING TOWARDS STAINES BRIDGE FROM THE HYTHE *c.1936*

The house on the left still stands on the corner of Farmers Road. The road to the left connected The Causeway through The Hythe to Old Chertsey Lane. The Lagonda works can just be seen in the distance. In 1937 a small bypass road linking Staines Bridge directly to Chertsey Lane and avoiding The Hythe was built. The area is now levelled and realigned to the present roundabout.

HYTHE ROUNDABOUT *1949*

The reorganisation and improving of roads begun in the 1930s, continued after the Second World War. Here, where the Hythe Roundabout is under construction, was once an orchard. On both sides of Thorpe Road can be seen the old Lagonda factory. The house between the roundabout and the factory was part of Ironbarks, home of John Goring, butcher and landowner of Staines. The house was used for offices, including those for W. O. Bentley and his team who designed the later Lagonda cars. To the west of Staines Bridge can be seen the emergency structure, known locally as the 'Bailey Bridge'. It was erected during the Second World War for general use should Staines Bridge be breached by bombing. The boathouse to the left of the cinema car-park in Staines has gone and it and part of the car park are now a restaurant.

P1417

P1424

P3080

P3081

THE HYTHE *c.1950*

'Huthe' or in modern form 'Hythe' means a landing place and such was Egham's picturesque street at the southern end of Staines Bridge. It was the home or lodging place of fishermen, bargemen, and a few farmers until recent times. The crinolined lady in the photograph attracted visitors into the Sunnyside Cafe. Next to the terrace of 18th century cottages with tile-hung walls is the ancient Swan inn where one bargeman killed another in 1678. The Hythe linked The Causeway from Egham to the old bridges. The southern abutment of the first stone bridge can be seen on the riverside near the Swan inn. The present Anne Boleyn hotel was a family home until 1927 and known as The Old Bridge House. The name 'Hythe' also applied to one of the Egham tithe divisions and later to an electoral ward and to the new Egham Hythe parish. The whole area was subject to flooding and little development occurred until this century, when, with hopes of better river control and the sale by the Crown of Royal Hythe Farm, major housing and industrial expansion was allowed.

ROYAL HYTHE FARM *1925*

Before the Enclosure Act for Egham in 1814 the farm consisted of scattered areas extending from Thorpe to the Glanty, and held under Crown Lease by Edgell Wyatt Edgell of Milton Park, and his forbears. The farmhouse of the mid-18th century still stands at The Hythe. The enclosure consolidated the scattered holdings into a single area of almost 200 acres fronting the Thorpe Road. In 1835 the lease of Wyatt Edgell reverted to the Crown and the farm became the Royal Hythe Farm. Here HRH The Prince of Wales, later HM King Edward VIII and later still HRH The Duke of Windsor, is seen talking to Mr Harry Few, the farmer, and Major Giles Loder at a Hunt Meeting in 1925. Hythe Field Avenue was built on this site.

ROYAL HYTHE FARMHOUSE *1925*

Between 1839 and 1841 a new farmstead was built for Henry Simmons, son of Thomas and Jane, the architect being Henry Rhodes. After 1846, Henry Simmons' son, Edward, left the farm and the subsequent tenants were the Adams, Saunders, Few, and finally Greenwood families. Miss Gladys Few, a daughter of the last but one tenant, is seen with her mother, Mrs Harry Few, outside the farmhouse. In 1953 the Royal Hythe Farm was sold by the Crown to Margaret Faulkner of London for £12,000. Later the area containing the house and buildings was purchased and Magna Carta School built on the site.

P3076

ROYAL HYTHE FARM MILK CART *c.1925*

Tom Few of the Royal Hythe Farm delivered milk from the churn all round the district, even as far afield as Chertsey.

P174

P1130

EGHAM HOSPITAL FETE *1907*

This grand fete was held in the grounds of Runnymede Park by kind permission of J. R. Fitzgerald Esq and Mr R. Clarke. The daylight fireworks shown here included a scene of a hospital ward with bed, patient and nurse attending. They were made by Messrs Pain and Son of London. Other attractions included W. Beach's roundabouts and swing boats; exhibition drill and tilting the bucket by Staines and Egham Fire Brigades; a military tournament by the 1st (King's) Dragoon Guards; Egham Town and Egham and Englefield Green Public Brass Bands and not least, sports. You had to find your own wheelbarrow for the wheelbarrow race. The admission prices, 1s (5p) for adults, 6d (2½p) for children and 2s 6d (12½p) for carriages aided the Hospital Saturday Fund, one of the many Friendly Societies that supported the working man and his family when sickness or injury kept him from work.

EGHAM COTTAGE HOSPITAL   1914-18

Egham's hospital was opened in 1880 in New Egham, now part of Englefield Green. It was run by a committee of local people and maintained by voluntary contributions. In the picture a group of patients, service and civilan, are seen sitting in the hospital garden. With them are the staff of the time: the matron, second from the right and the gardener, second from the left. The Cottage Hospital closed in December 1985 on safety grounds.

P144A

THE GREAT WAR   *1914-18*

Private Percy Higgs, seen on the right in the picture, learnt to drive in all kinds of weather on Egham Hill even when it was covered in ice and snow. At the beginning of the war he left his job as a counting-house clerk with the Army and Navy Stores and his wife and child in Peckham Rye to join the Royal Army Service Corps. His duties involved taking the service mail from Mount Pleasant to the London Docks and collecting and delivering food for the Army camps. Towards the end of his life, Mr Higgs returned to Egham, the district he had known as a soldier. Dennis Bros of Guildford manufactured lorries for the War Office during the First World War.

P3082

P1067A

VISITING THE CANADIAN LUMBER CAMP   *between 1914-18*

Egham and Englefield Green were hosts to a Canadian lumber camp during the Great War. Men and women from the Camp were billeted in the town and local families visited the Camp. Seen here standing in the doorway are Sergeant Schofield with his sister, Miss Schofield on the left, and on the right Miss Olive Osman. This scene of tranquility must have been a far cry for the soldiers from the horrors of the trenches.

63 HIGH STREET *1940*

Egham, though considered safe enough to take in evacuees, did not escape aerial attack in the Second World War. Bombs fell on the district in the autumn of 1940, a fatal incident occurring at Arkell's drapery shop in the High Street on 16 November. Two boys, evacuated to Strode's from Raine's Foundation School in Stepney, East London and billeted with Mrs Arkell, were killed. The young daughter of the family also perished.

P1040A

MULLENS ROAD *1941*

More tragedies were to come. At 7.30pm on 9 January 1941, during an enemy air raid, the open country between Milton Park and Egham Hythe was lit up as bright as day by 200-300 magnesium incendiary bombs. A minute or two later Egham was shaken by the crash of an explosion as a heavy bomb fell in Mullens Road, Pooley Green. About 22 steel-framed council houses were destroyed, eight persons being killed and about eighteen injured. A crater about 34ft wide and 15ft deep was made and gas, light, water and sewer lines broken. Altogether about 100 other houses received superficial damage.

P1142

EGHAM HIGH STREET *1941*

Two months later Egham held a War Weapons Week. Taking the salute outside the Fire Station was Lt-Gen T. R. Eastwood, Chief of the Home Guard. The leading band is seen here passing the saluting base. In the background is the International Stores. The procession took three-quarters of an hour to pass the saluting base. All fighting services were included in the procession, both vehicular and fighting units. The Egham Fire Service squad was represented as well as a contingent from the Calgary Highlanders complete with pipe band.

P1142

EGHAM FIRE STATION   *1941*

Egham hoped to raise £100,000 for the war effort in that week. The indicator was mounted on the 54ft hose drying tower at the Fire Station. The figure of the medieval baron was 8ft tall and was wound up every evening during the 'Week' to show the takings up to that time. All publicity work and the composing of such slogans as 'Every copper helps to arrest Hitler' were the responsibility of Mr Spiller, Publicity Manager of the British American Tobacco Co, operating from Rusham House in Whitehall Lane.

P1142

EGHAM AMBULANCE STATION   *1941*

During the Second World War many civilians became part-time volunteers in support of the Civil Defence. Here is a group of Ambulance Drivers and Attendants of the Egham Detachment, British Red Cross. Their leader, Miss Taylor, is in the centre of the picture.

P1142

AIR RAID PRECAUTIONS AMBULANCE   1941

As will be noted, this is a private car chassis with the rear of the body part cut away and a special lightweight body built on. It accommodated four stretcher cases but this type of vehicle needed careful handling as it was inclined to sway dangerously on corners. The Girl Guides undertook to keep the ambulances clean.

P1142

EGHAM HIGH STREET   1941

Private cars were also available and carried four stretchers each. This vehicle, especially designed by the Stanley Engineering Co of Egham, makers of the Argson Invalid Tricycle, was presented to the Egham Branch of the St John's Ambulance Association. It could carry a single stretcher case and a sitting case in an emergency. In 1941 time was running out for the Registry Office for Servants. Its board survives in The Egham Museum.

P1142

RIVER THAMES   *aerial view*   c.1950

There is evidence of Bronze Age settlements relatively close to the river. In Saxon times the Thames was a boundary between the Kingdom of Wessex on the south and Mercia to the north. The small medieval town of Egham grew up on the slightly higher ground above the river. Until the coming of the turnpike roads and later the railways, the river was a major highway between London and Oxford for the transport not only of all manner of cargoes but also a cheap means of passenger transport. In 1828 the standard fare per person to be rowed from London Bridge to Egham Hythe was 2s 6d (12½p). In 1929 the meadows of Runnymede were 'gladly offered to the nation' by the widow and sons of Urban Hanlow Broughton, Lord Fairhaven, in his 'Perpetual Memory', as the commemorative pillars record. The lodges at the centre front of this picture, designed by Sir Edward Lutyens, mark the beginning of Long Mead with Runnymede beyond.

P2548

HAYMAKING ON RUNNYMEDE

The Meads themselves, being regularly flooded, have always provided lush pasture for Egham farmers. Another thriving local industry with a prosperous export market until the 1880s was the growing of withies. Withies are the canes grown from pollarded willows and are used in basket making. The most important beds were on the river banks near the present Runnymede Bridge, between the river and The Causway and from The Hythe to Penton Hook.

P2323

Bell Weir Lock, Egham. W 1010

BELL WEIR LOCK *looking upstream c.1905*

Attempts to control the flow of the river were constantly made. In 1811 discussions for a new Egham lock were held, the suggested site being between Ankerwyke Island and Milsom's Point. In view of vehement local oppositioin, however, the present position was adopted. The lock and weir opened in the winter of 1817-18 at a cost of £6,650, with Charles Bell the lock's first keeper lending it his name. Ten years later the weir was 'blown up' by an accumulation of ice. The lock and weir were rebuilt in 1867-68 and again in 1877. In Edwardian times 'messing about on the river' was a favourite pastime, with the punt a particularly popular mode of recreation.

P139A

P2174D

RUNNYMEDE *looking upstream* *1955*

The Meads and river banks have also long been a source of pleasure to the public. In the 18th and 19th centuries Runnymede was the site of the then renowned Egham Races, attended by royalty and drawing large crowds. The coming of the railway to Egham and Staines brought 'beanfeasters' or day-trippers to the river bank in large numbers. In the early 1930s the London Transport 117E bus from Hounslow to Slough was routed via Runnymede on Saturdays. After the Second World War, with more people driving motor cars, the river became accessible to even more visitors as this photograph, taken on the last Saturday in July 1955, shows.

P1267

RUNNYMEDE PAGEANT   *1934*

Runnymede is most well known, of course, as the site of the sealing of Magna Carta by King John in 1215. This scene was re-enacted in 1934, appropriately enough by the people of Egham and Wraysbury. Eight episodes from the *History of Britain Through the Ages* made up the pageant, probably the most lavish of the era. The historic meadow had been donated to The National Trust just a few years earlier. The pageant received royal patronage from HRH The Prince of Wales, later HM King Edward VIII and later still HRH The Duke of Windsor, and TRH The Duke and Duchess of York (later HM King George VI and HM Queen Elizabeth). However, as the pageant took place during Ascot week no royalty actually attended.

P1168H

RUNNYMEDE PAGEANT   *1934*

'A Tournament at Windsor given by Edward III in 1358' was presented by the Windsor Group. The pageant was the brainchild of Lady Enid de Chair of Podenhale, Virginia Water, to raise money for local charities. She invited the famous pageant master, Gwen Lally, to produce the spectacle. Two performances were held daily, many local people took part and it was estimated that a total of over 90,000 people came to see it. Sadly, due to apparent ignorance of the tax laws, the pageant raised very little for local charities, but as a spectacle it was a huge success.

THEIR NAME LIVETH
FOR EVERMORE

P1692

AIR FORCES MEMORIAL   *Cooper's Hill*   *dedicated 1953*

The Memorial is dedicated to the fallen of the Air Forces of the British Commonwealth who operated from bases in the United Kingdom and North West Europe in the Second World War and who have no known grave. The memorial was unveiled by Her Majesty Queen Elizabeth II on 17 October 1953, only a few months after her coronation. The site for the Memorial, on the very crest of Cooper's Hill, was the gift of Sir Eugen and Lady Effie Millington-Drake. Sir Edward Maufe was the architect, and the material Portland stone. Avenues of silver birches lead to the entrance. Within are quiet lawns and on either side arcaded cloisters where the missing airmen's names are inscribed. The square tower of the shrine is surmounted by an Air Force crown and a single star, clearly visible from below. The vast window, that overlooks the river, is engraved with words from Psalm CXXXIX: 'If I climb up into heaven thou art there . . . If I take the wings of the morning . . . even there also shall thy hand lead me.' On either side of the tower are small look-outs, giving magnificent views over the trees and meadows towards Windsor and over the river to Heathrow. At the unveiling ceremony Her Majesty quoted the lines of Alexander Pope: 'On Cooper's Hill eternal wreaths shall grow, While lasts the mountain or while Thames shall flow.' Indeed, the niches in the cloisters are rarely without the tribute of flowers and loving messages.

P3085

THE AMERICAN BAR ASSOCIATION MONUMENT   *1957*

The name Runnymede is synonymous throughout the English-speaking world with constitutional freedom. The significance of the sealing of the Great Charter there by King John in 1215 has particularly captured the imagination of many citizens of the United States of America. In July 1957 the American Bar Association dedicated this elegant little rotunda, on the slopes above Runnymede, as 'a tribute to Magna Carta, symbol of freedom under law'.

THE DEDICATION OF THE JOHN F. KENNEDY MEMORIAL   *1965*

It was fitting that the place chosen as the memorial to the assassinated American President should be a piece of English woodland and meadow just above Runnymede. The memorial itself, carved from a seven-ton block of Portland stone, in its setting of trees and path of granite sets, was designed by Mr G. A. Jellicoe. Present at the dedication with HM The Queen and HRH The Duke of Edinburgh were the late President's brothers, Robert and Edward, two of his sisters, his widow, Mrs Jacqueline Kennedy and his children, Caroline and John.

P3084

P1574